FOLGER McKINSEY ELEMENTARY SCHOOL

REVIEW COPY
COURTESY OF
ENSLOW PUBLISHERS, INC

Tools

Search

Notes

Discuss

MyReportLinks.com Books

Go!

PRESIDENTS

FRANKLIN PIERCE

A MyReportLinks.com Book

Jeff C. Young

MyReportLinks.com Books
an imprint of

Enslow Publishers, Inc. E
Box 398, 40 Industrial Road
Berkeley Heights, NJ 07922
USA

FOLGER McKINSEY ELEMENTARY SCHOOL

MyReportLinks.com Books, an imprint of Enslow Publishers, Inc.

Copyright © 2002 by Enslow Publishers, Inc.

All rights reserved.

No part of this book may be reproduced by any means
without the written permission of the publisher.

Library of Congress Cataloging-in-Publication Data

Young, Jeff C., 1948 –
     Franklin Pierce / Jeff C. Young.
        p. cm. — (Presidents)
     Includes bibliographical references and index.
     Summary: A biography of the New Hampshire politician who served as
president during a period of increasing bitterness between the North
and the South. Includes Internet links to Web sites, source documents,
and photographs related to Franklin Pierce.
     ISBN 0-7660-5073-4
     1. Pierce, Franklin, 1804–1869—Juvenile literature. 2.
Presidents—United States—Biography—Juvenile literature. [1. Pierce,
Franklin, 1804–1869. 2. Presidents.] I. Title. II. Series.
   E432.Y68 2002
   973.6'6'092—dc21
   [B]
                                                    2001004303

Printed in the United States of America

10 9 8 7 6 5 4 3 2 1

To Our Readers:
Through the purchase of this book, you and your library gain access to the Report Links that specifically back up this book.
The Publisher will provide access to the Report Links that back up this book and will keep these Report Links up to date on **www.myreportlinks.com** for three years from the book's first publication date.
We have done our best to make sure all Internet addresses in this book were active and appropriate when we went to press. However, the author and the Publisher have no control over, and assume no liability for, the material available on those Internet sites or on other Web sites they may link to.
The usage of the MyReportLinks.com Books Web site is subject to the terms and conditions stated on the Usage Policy Statement on **www.myreportlinks.com**.
In the future, a password may be required to access the Report Links that back up this book. The password is found on the bottom of page 4 of this book.
Any comments or suggestions can be sent by e-mail to comments@myreportlinks.com or to the address on the back cover.

Photo Credits: © Corel Corporation, pp. 1 (background), 3; Courtesy of © 2001 National Museum of American History, Smithsonian Institution, pp. 16, 33; Courtesy of ADAH Alabama Department of Archives & History, p. 29; Courtesy of American Memory/Library of Congress, p. 34; Courtesy of Lane Memorial Library, p. 44; Courtesy of MyReportLinks.com Books, p. 4; Courtesy of PBS Online, p. 22; Courtesy of The Papers of Jefferson Davis, p. 32; Courtesy of the White House Home Page, p. 39; Courtesy of the White House Historical Association, p. 41; Department of the Interior, p. 28; *Dictionary of American Portraits,* Dover Publications, Inc., © 1967, pp. 15, 20, 26; Library of Congress, pp. 1, 17, 23, 27, 43; National Archives, pp. 12, 37.

Cover Photo: © Corel Corporation (background); White House Collection, Courtesy White House Historical Association.

Contents

MyReportLinks.com Books
Great Books, Great Links, Great for Research!

MyReportLinks.com Books present the information you need to learn about your report subject. In addition, they show you where to go on the Internet for more information. The pre-evaluated Report Links that back up this book are kept up to date on **www.myreportlinks.com**. With the purchase of a MyReportLinks.com Books title, you and your library gain access to the Report Links that specifically back up that book. The Report Links save hours of research time and link to dozens—even hundreds—of Web sites, source documents, and photos related to your report topic.

Please see "To Our Readers" on the Copyright page for important information about this book, the MyReportLinks.com Books Web site, and the Report Links that back up this book.

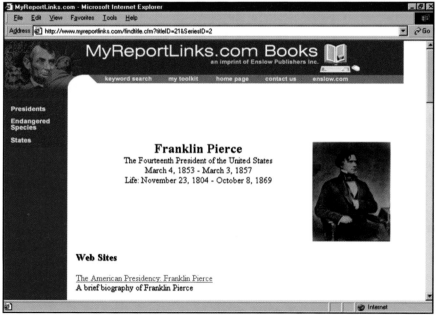

Access:

The Publisher will provide access to the Report Links that back up this book and will try to keep these Report Links up to date on our Web site for three years from the book's first publication date. Please enter **PPI17Y7** if asked for a password.

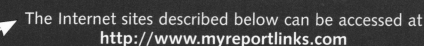

The Internet sites described below can be accessed at
http://www.myreportlinks.com

▶**The American Presidency: Franklin Pierce**   *EDITOR'S CHOICE
This site provides a comprehensive profile of Franklin Pierce. Here you
will find Pierce's inaugural address and quick facts about him.

Link to this Internet site from http://www.myreportlinks.com

▶**Franklin Pierce**   *EDITOR'S CHOICE
A quick-reference guide to the life and times of Franklin Pierce. Here
you will find a list of his cabinet members, notable events in his
administration, and historical documents.

Link to this Internet site from http://www.myreportlinks.com

▶**The White House History: Franklin Pierce**   *EDITOR'S CHOICE
This official White House Web site holds a brief biography of
Franklin Pierce.

Link to this Internet site from http://www.myreportlinks.com

▶**Objects from the Presidency**   *EDITOR'S CHOICE
By navigating through this site you will find objects related to all the
United States presidents, including Franklin Pierce. You can also read a
brief description of Pierce, the era he lived in, and learn about the
office of the presidency.

Link to this Internet site from http://www.myreportlinks.com

▶**Franklin Pierce: A Horse with No Name**   *EDITOR'S CHOICE
This brief summary describes Franklin Pierce's presidency. You will also
find a historical document and a video clip.

Link to this Internet site from http://www.myreportlinks.com

▶**American Presidents Life Portraits: Franklin Pierce**   *EDITOR'S CHOICE
This site provides life facts and trivia about Franklin Pierce. You can
also read a letter written by Pierce.

Link to this Internet site from http://www.myreportlinks.com

 The Internet sites described below can be accessed at
http://www.myreportlinks.com

▶**The American Presidency: Jane Pierce**
This brief biography of Jane Pierce tells that she was opposed to her husband's political career.

Link to this Internet site from http://www.myreportlinks.com

▶**An Act to Organize the Territories of Nebraska and Kansas**
This site holds the text of the Kansas-Nebraska Act. Learn about the act that allowed people in organized territories to decide for themselves whether to be a slave or free state.

Link to this Internet site from http://www.myreportlinks.com

▶**The Battle of Buena Vista: February 23, 1847**
America's Story from America's Library, a Library of Congress Web site, provides a brief overview of some key players in the Battle of Buena Vista. Franklin Pierce, a veteran of the Mexican War, defeated major General Winfield Scott in the election of 1852.

Link to this Internet site from http://www.myreportlinks.com

▶**The Border**
This site provides a detailed history of the border between the United States and Mexico. Here you will find time lines and a morphing map.

Link to this Internet site from http://www.myreportlinks.com

▶**Franklin Pierce (1804–1869)**
This site contains an interesting fact, a quote, and a brief biography of Franklin Pierce. You can also access Pierce's inaugural address.

Link to this Internet site from http://www.myreportlinks.com

▶**Franklin Pierce (1804–1869)**
From the National Portrait Gallery come two portraits of Franklin Pierce. The oil portrait was painted by George P. A. Healy in 1853.

Link to this Internet site from http://www.myreportlinks.com

Report Links

The Internet sites described below can be accessed at
http://www.myreportlinks.com

▶**Franklin Pierce: Fourteenth President**
Here you will find an overview of Franklin Pierce's life and
presidency as well as links to Pierce's inaugural address
and the 1852 election results.

Link to this Internet site from http://www.myreportlinks.com

▶**Franklin Pierce: Inaugural Address**
This site contains the full text of Franklin Pierce's inaugural address,
which he delivered on March 4, 1853.

Link to this Internet site from http://www.myreportlinks.com

▶**Franklin Pierce's Obituary**
This site holds the obituary of Franklin Pierce, as it appeared in the
New York Times on October 9, 1869.

Link to this Internet site from http://www.myreportlinks.com

▶**Franklin Pierce: The Shadow President**
Here you will find a brief overview of Pierce's presidency as well as a
detailed biography of his life before, during, and after his presidency.
A great place to begin your research.

Link to this Internet site from http://www.myreportlinks.com

▶**The Gadsden Purchase**
At this site you will learn about the Gadsden Purchase, the key players,
and the disputed land.

Link to this Internet site from http://www.myreportlinks.com

▶**"I Do Solemnly Swear..."**
This site brings to life the inauguration of Franklin Pierce with a
collection of items. Here you will find a portrait of Pierce, engravings
of the ceremonies, and copies of his address.

Link to this Internet site from http://www.myreportlinks.com

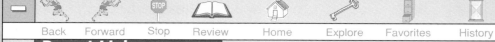
 The Internet sites described below can be accessed at
http://www.myreportlinks.com

▶ **Jane Appleton Pierce**
Learn about the life of Jane Appleton Pierce, and her marriage to
Franklin Pierce.

Link to this Internet site from http://www.myreportlinks.com

▶ **Jefferson Davis Chronology**
This site offers a detailed time line of the life of Jefferson Davis, who served as
secretary of war under Franklin Pierce.

Link to this Internet site from http://www.myreportlinks.com

▶ **Likeness of New Hampshire War Heroes & Personages**
Here you will learn about Franklin Pierce's rise from private to brigadier
general during the Mexican War.

Link to this Internet site from http://www.myreportlinks.com

▶ **The Ostend Manifesto**
This site contains the text to the Ostend Manifesto.

Link to this Internet site from http://www.myreportlinks.com

▶ **Pierce, Franklin**
At encyclopedia.com you will find a brief profile of Franklin Pierce, and view
the basic facts of Pierce's life and administration.

Link to this Internet site from http://www.myreportlinks.com

▶ **Pierce, Franklin**
This site provides a brief profile of Franklin Pierce where you will learn about
his life and rise to the presidency.

Link to this Internet site from http://www.myreportlinks.com

➤ The Internet sites described below can be accessed at
http://www.myreportlinks.com

▶**Portsmouth Harbor Trail: Franklin Pierce in Friendly Port**
This site provides an account of Franklin Pierce's visit to Portsmouth,
New Hampshire, in 1856.

Link to this Internet site from http://www.myreportlinks.com

▶**The Progress Report: The Gadsden Purchase**
This site contains an overview of the Gadsden Purchase. Here you will
learn about the purchase that would help complete a transcontinental
railroad line.

Link to this Internet site from http://www.myreportlinks.com

▶**The U.S.-Mexican War**
Learn about the Mexican War, where Franklin Pierce achieved the rank
of brigadier general.

Link to this Internet site from http://www.myreportlinks.com

▶**The White House Historical Association**
By navigating through this site you will find information on all the
presidents of the United States, including Franklin Pierce. You can also
take a virtual tour of the White House.

Link to this Internet site from http://www.myreportlinks.com

▶**The White House History: Jane Means Appleton**
The official White House Web site holds the biography of Jane
Pierce. Here you will learn how Jane felt about her husband being
involved in politics.

Link to this Internet site from http://www.myreportlinks.com

▶**Who is William Rufus King?**
At this site you will learn about William Rufus King, Franklin Pierce's
vice president. King was the only national public official to be sworn in
on foreign soil.

Link to this Internet site from http://www.myreportlinks.com

Highlights

1804—*Nov. 23:* Born in Hillsborough, New Hampshire.

1824—*Sep. 1:* Graduates from Bowdoin College in Brunswick, Maine.

1827—*Sep.:* Admitted to the New Hampshire bar, the state's association of lawyers.

1831—Elected speaker of the house in the New Hampshire legislature.

1832—Elected to the U.S. House of Representatives and serves until 1837.

1834—*Nov. 19:* Marries Jane Means Appleton in Amherst, New Hampshire.

1836—Elected to the U.S. Senate and serves until 1842.

　　　　—*Feb. 2:* Son, Franklin Pierce, is born, but dies three days later.

1839—*Aug. 27:* Son, Frank Robert Pierce, is born.

1841—*April 13:* Son, Benjamin Pierce, is born.

　　　　—*Nov. 14:* Frank Robert Pierce dies.

1847–1848—Serves in the U.S. Army during Mexican War, achieving rank of brigadier general.

1852—Elected president of the United States.

1853–1857—Serves as the fourteenth president of the United States.

1853—Gadsden Purchase acquires remainder of land that eventually becomes the forty-eight contiguous states.

　　　　—*Jan. 6:* Benjamin Pierce dies in a railroad accident.

1854—Kansas-Nebraska Act allows for people in organized territories to decide for themselves whether to be a slave or free state.

1856—The Democratic Party chooses not to renominate Pierce for president.

　　　　—*Sep. 4:* First time an American flag is flown in Japan.

1863—*Dec. 2:* Wife, Jean Means Appleton Pierce, dies.

1865—*April:* Pierce is confronted by a mob of townspeople, angry that he was not flying a flag to mourn the death of President Lincoln.

1869—*Oct. 8:* Franklin Pierce dies in Concord, New Hampshire.

Chapter 1 ▶

Where is the Flag?, 1865

When the residents of Concord, New Hampshire, heard that President Abraham Lincoln had been assassinated, they were shocked, stunned, and angered.

A mass meeting was held in the town square. A mob of men and boys formed. For the next two hours, they visited the residences, stores, and shops of Concord. The angry throng of three hundred to six hundred people uttered threats against homes and businesses that were not flying the United States flag. In at least one instance, they drove a woman from her home.

Emboldened by their power, the mob decided to visit the home of ex-President Franklin Pierce. Pierce was a convenient target, because he had opposed the outbreak of the war and Lincoln's war policies.

Pierce was relaxing at home when a servant warned him that a noisy crowd was approaching. He only had a few moments to get ready to face them. He opened his front door and calmly surveyed the rowdy crowd. They demanded a speech. Pierce denounced the assassination and condemned the assassin. Soon someone yelled: "Where is your flag?"[1]

Now the ex-president found his patriotism questioned. He was quick to reply. Although he was frail and weak at sixty years old, his voice was clear and strong.

"It is not necessary for me to show my devotions for the Stars and Stripes by any special exhibition upon the demand of any man or body of men . . ."[2]

America's fourteenth president reminded the crowd of his devoted service to his state and nation as a state legislator, army general, congressman, senator, and president.

"If the period which I have served our state and country in various situations, commencing more than thirty-five years ago, has left the question of my devotion to the flag, the constitution and the Union in doubt, it is too late now to resume it by any such exhibition."[3]

Pierce finished his impromptu speech and the crowd quietly left. The speaking skills that had swayed juries, persuaded politicians, and charmed voters had turned away and silenced an angry mob.

Unfortunately for Pierce, making speeches was much easier than leading a nation divided by slavery and destined to endure a horrendous civil war. Elected by an overwhelming electoral mandate in 1852, Pierce would be denied renomination by his party in 1856. After leaving the presidency, Pierce would find himself scorned, snubbed, and largely forgotten by the country he unselfishly served.

Abraham Lincoln was assassinated on April 14, 1865.

Formative Years, 1804–1827

Franklin Pierce was raised in a household immersed in politics and steeped in patriotism. His father, Benjamin Pierce, was a Revolutionary War veteran who fought in the battles of Bunker Hill and Saratoga. After the war, Benjamin Pierce entered politics and eventually served two terms as governor of New Hampshire.

▶ Young Franklin

Franklin was the sixth of eight children born to Benjamin and Anna Kendrick Pierce. He was born on November 23, 1804, at the family's log cabin in Hillsborough, New Hampshire. Shortly after Franklin's birth, the Pierces moved into a roomy house that Benjamin built. The house also served as an inn and tavern. Young Franklin would eagerly listen to news of the outside world from the travelers, drinkers, and guests.

Franklin was a handsome boy with curly black hair and dark gray eyes. He was an energetic child who played hard and worked even harder. He learned how to hunt, fish, and fire a gun. He also learned reading, writing, and arithmetic. Benjamin Pierce had never attended school longer than three weeks a year. He was determined that his children would receive a good education.

▶ Education

Along with a love of learning, Franklin Pierce developed a love for his country. He had a near reverence for the military

and yearned to someday command troops in battle. He was spellbound by heroic tales of the Revolutionary War told to him by his father.

When he was twelve, Franklin began attending Hancock Academy, a private school a few miles from his home. While attending Hancock, he openly defied his father. He was terribly homesick and felt he did not need any more schooling. After all, he already had more education than his father. One Sunday morning, Franklin snuck off campus and walked home. When he arrived, his parents were at church. When Benjamin Pierce returned home, he did not act surprised to see his son. Franklin explained why he was home. His father was not angry. He asked his runaway son to stay for dinner.

Franklin felt that he had persuaded his father to let him quit school. That feeling ended after dinner when he saw his father hitching up the wagon. Benjamin Pierce ordered Franklin on to the wagon and began taking him back to the school. When they got about halfway there, his father ordered him off the wagon and told him to walk the rest of the way.

Before completing the three- to four-mile walk, Pierce got caught in a heavy rain. He arrived at the school, downcast and drenched. Apparently, he never openly defied his father again.

▶ Breaking the Rules

In the fall of 1820, Pierce entered Bowdoin College in Brunswick, Maine. Life there was strict. Students were there to learn, not to party or socialize. The college had strict rules prohibiting drinking, attending plays, gambling, singing, and shouting. Students were not allowed to go into the town of Brunswick or to leave their rooms on Saturday and Sunday nights.

Pierce broke most of the rules, but he got away with it. He would cut classes to go wandering through the Maine woods or to go swimming in a cold, saltwater lake. He would also frequent a tavern that was supposed to be off-limits to students. That is probably where his longtime problems with alcohol abuse began. He would also visit an old woman who told fortunes with playing cards and tea leaves.

During his second year of college, Pierce became more outgoing and started making some friends. Two of his new friends were Nathaniel Hawthorne and Zenas Caldwell. Hawthorne would later become one of America's best-known writers and Pierce's biographer. Caldwell would become a noted Methodist clergyman.

While he was succeeding socially, Pierce continued to neglect his studies. He remained an indifferent student, content to just get by. He had no scruples about copying assignments from cooperative classmates. Early in his junior year, he ranked last in his

Pierce's friend, ▶ author Nathaniel Hawthorne.

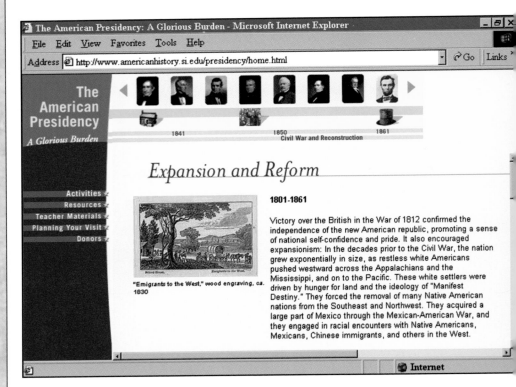

The American Presidency
A Glorious Burden

1841

1850
Civil War and Reconstruction

1861

Activities
Resources
Teacher Materials
Planning Your Visit
Donors

Expansion and Reform

"Emigrants to the West," wood engraving, ca. 1830

1801-1861

Victory over the British in the War of 1812 confirmed the independence of the new American republic, promoting a sense of national self-confidence and pride. It also encouraged expansionism: In the decades prior to the Civil War, the nation grew exponentially in size, as restless white Americans pushed westward across the Appalachians and the Mississippi, and on to the Pacific. These white settlers were driven by hunger for land and the ideology of "Manifest Destiny." They forced the removal of many Native American nations from the Southeast and Northwest. They acquired a large part of Mexico through the Mexican-American War, and they engaged in racial encounters with Native Americans, Mexicans, Chinese immigrants, and others in the West.

Franklin Pierce supported President Andrew Jackson's opinions on many issues, especially those regarding Manifest Destiny and the Indian Removal Act. Under the Indian Removal Act, many American Indian nations from the Southwest and Northwest were uprooted.

class academically. The class standings were a wake-up call for him.

An Abrupt Change

Under the positive influence of his friends, Caldwell and Hawthorne, Pierce changed his ways. He quit cutting classes and began attending chapel services. He stopped coming to class unprepared. At the end of his senior year, he ranked fifth in his class and was chosen to be the commencement speaker.

After graduating from Bowdoin in the summer of 1824, Pierce returned to Hillsborough, New Hampshire. Benjamin Pierce was working as the local postmaster. He turned the job over to Franklin. When he was not delivering mail on horseback, Franklin Pierce studied law in the office of a local attorney.

In November 1824, John Quincy Adams won a hotly contested presidential election. The Pierces were fervent supporters of Adams's opponent, Andrew Jackson. Their support cost them the postmaster's position. Franklin had to find other work. He moved to Portsmouth and began working as a law clerk.

In 1826, Benjamin Pierce became the Democratic nominee for governor of New Hampshire. He lost by just about five thousand votes, but the loss built a foundation for future victories. One year later, Benjamin Pierce was elected governor by a landslide vote. Six months later, Franklin finished his law studies and began practicing law in an office built by his father. Now he was ready to take after Benjamin Pierce and enter politics.

Pierce's father was the biggest single influence on his political beliefs. Benjamin Pierce was a staunch Anti-Federalist and supporter of Thomas Jefferson and Andrew Jackson. The Anti-Federalists believed in a strict interpretation of the Constitution and strong state governments, rather

President Andrew Jackson. ▶

than a strong federal government. Under Jefferson's leadership, the Anti-Federalists changed their name to the Democratic-Republican Party.

After the election of 1828, the Democratic-Republican Party shortened its name to the Democratic Party. The party still strongly supported states' rights. Its supporters included small farmers, frontiersmen, and debtors. Benjamin Pierce was twice elected governor of New Hampshire running on Democratic ideals.

Politician & Attorney, 1828–1851

Bolstered by his father's good reputation, Pierce began building a successful law practice. Success in law led to success in politics. In May 1828, he was appointed justice of the peace. The next year, he was elected to the state legislature. After being reelected in 1831, his fellow lawmakers elected him speaker of the house. At the age of twenty-six, he was presiding over 238 other representatives.

Pierce enjoyed socializing with his fellow lawmakers. Sometimes he enjoyed it a bit too much. Many of the backwoods legislators were hard drinking men, and he would try to match them drink for drink. Although he would sometimes drink too much, the drinking did not seem to keep him from being an effective speaker.

▶ Entering Politics

In 1832, Andrew Jackson was reelected to a second term as president. Pierce traveled throughout New Hampshire and Massachusetts campaigning for Jackson. Jackson won easily and Pierce's popularity reached new heights. Some New Hampshire newspapers were calling him the most popular man in the state. Democratic Party leaders took notice of his immense popularity and nominated him to run for Congress.

Pierce was elected to Congress in 1832. He was reelected two years later. During his four years in the House of Representatives, Pierce consistently supported President Jackson. He backed the president's campaign against

maintaining the Bank of the United States. They believed it only served the interests of wealthy eastern investors instead of the common working people. Pierce also wholeheartedly supported President Jackson's opposition to spending federal funds for internal improvements such as roads and canals. Pierce and his fellow congressional Democrats felt that the individual states should pay for their own improvements.

While serving in the House, Pierce also defended slavery. He denounced abolitionists (people who wanted to make slavery illegal) as "reckless fanatics." He also supported a legislative practice known as the gag rule, which prevented the House of Representatives from considering antislavery petitions.

▶ Marriage and Family

Since he seemingly had a secure future in politics and law, Pierce began thinking about getting married and starting a family. On November 19, 1834, he married twenty-eight-year-old Jane Means Appleton. When and where they first met is not known. Perhaps it was through her brother-in-law, Alpheus S. Packard, who was one of Pierce's college instructors.

Franklin and Jane seemed an unlikely couple. She was

◀ *Jane Means Appleton Pierce.*

shy, frail, and reserved. Franklin was outgoing, congenial, and high-spirited. They truly loved each other, but they often quarreled. Jane never cared for politics or the Washington social scene. Yet, they remained together until her death in 1863.

In 1836, the New Hampshire legislature elected Pierce to the U.S. Senate. Prior to the passage of the Seventeenth Amendment in 1913, state legislatures elected U.S. Senators. He took his seat in March 1837. At age thirty-two, Pierce was the Senate's youngest member.

As a senator, Pierce usually remained loyal to his party. He supported most of the programs of Jackson's successor, President Martin Van Buren. Pierce continued to oppose federal funding for internal improvements, and was still unwavering in his support of slavery. He staunchly opposed efforts to abolish slavery in the District of Columbia and in American territories. He is said to have felt that the Constitution "safeguarded property rights in slavery for all time."[1]

▶ A Break from Politics

In 1840, President Van Buren was defeated for reelection by the Whig candidate, William Henry Harrison. Harrison's popularity allowed the Whigs to gain control of both houses of Congress. Now that the Democrats were the minority party, Pierce began losing interest in Senate business. Jane continually asked him to give up politics. Pierce finally gave in to her wishes. In February 1842, he resigned his Senate seat and returned to Concord.

Even after returning to his law practice, Pierce was unable to completely give up politics. He served as state chairman of the New Hampshire Democratic Party. In 1844, he directed the presidential campaign of James K.

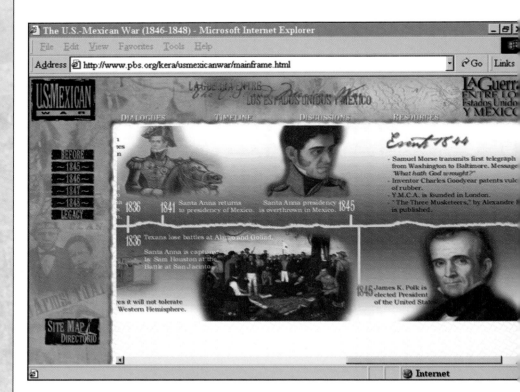

The U.S.-Mexican War (1846-1848) - Microsoft Internet Explorer

File   Edit   View   Favorites   Tools   Help

Address http://www.pbs.org/kera/usmexicanwar/mainframe.html   Go   Links

Events 1844

- Samuel Morse transmits first telegraph from Washington to Baltimore. Message "What hath God wrought?"
- Inventor Charles Goodyear patents vulc of rubber.
- Y.M.C.A. is founded in London.
- "The Three Musketeers," by Alexandre is published.

1836   1841 Santa Anna returns to presidency of Mexico.

Santa Anna presidency is overthrown in Mexico. 1845

1836 Texans lose battles at Alamo and Goliad.

Santa Anna is captured by Sam Houston at the Battle at San Jacinto.

...es it will not tolerate Western Hemisphere.

1845 James K. Polk is elected President of the United States.

▲ *Pierce fought in the Mexican War from 1846 to 1848. In hopes of living up to his father's tales of courage, Pierce enlisted with the volunteer regiment in Concord. He was forced to resign from his post because of injury and illness.*

Polk in New Hampshire. After Polk was elected, Pierce was rewarded by being appointed the U.S. district attorney for New Hampshire.

▶ The Mexican War

The only thing that completely diverted Pierce's attention from politics was his participation in the Mexican War from 1846 to 1848. In May 1846, he enlisted as a private with the volunteer regiment in Concord. After a few months of service, Pierce was commissioned a colonel in the regular army. Sometime in March 1847, he was promoted to brigadier general. He hoped to emulate his father's record of battlefield heroism, but injuries and illness prevented that.

At the Battle of Contreras, an artillery shell exploded close to Pierce's horse. The frightened horse reared, stumbled, and fell. Pierce was slammed so hard into the pommel of the saddle, he passed out from the pain. He also wrenched his knee. A few days later, he reinjured the knee in another battle. During the decisive Battle of Chapultepec, General Pierce was sick with dysentery. In February 1848, he resigned from his commission.

▶ Return to Concord

After returning to Concord, Pierce achieved much prominence as a trial lawyer. He swayed juries by combining his brilliant speaking skills with a shrewd sense of how his words were affecting his audience. As his biographer, Roy Franklin Nichols, noted: "He didn't convince juries, he converted them."[2]

Franklin Pierce ▶
as president.

Even when he was trying cases, politics was an important part of Pierce's life. New Hampshire Democrats offered him the nomination for governor, but he declined. Pierce thought he was through running for office, but he was wrong. A badly divided Democratic Party would make Pierce their presidential candidate in 1852.

Chapter 4

Dark Horse Candidate, 1852

With the 1852 presidential election approaching, Pierce was an unlikely candidate. There were already several declared candidates vying for the Democratic presidential nomination. Senator Stephen A. Douglas from Illinois; former U.S. Secretary of State James Buchanan; former Democratic nominee Lewis Cass; and New York politician William Marcy were all seeking the nomination. Pierce also had the disadvantage of being from a small New England state. New Hampshire had never produced a president or presidential nominee.

The last New Englander to be elected president had been John Quincy Adams in 1824. Pierce was not well known outside of New England, and he had not held office since leaving the Senate in 1842.

▶ A Cryptic Reply

Still, Pierce had several things in his favor. He was one of the party's best orators, and he had a solid record of winning elections. Because of his charming and affable personality, he had few enemies. Although he served without distinction, he was a war veteran. Most importantly, he was a Northerner who could win votes in the South because he was not an abolitionist and was not against slavery expanding into the territories seeking statehood.

In April 1852, a group of Mexican War officers led by Caleb Cushing and Gideon J. Pillow met in Washington.

They discussed Pierce as a compromise candidate. Then, they wrote to him and asked him to commit himself as a candidate.

Pierce answered with a cryptic reply. He wrote that it was up to his friends to determine ". . . what is my duty and what may be the best interest of the party."[1]

Being a cagey politician, he did not say yes, but he did not say no. Pillow and Cushing continued to drum up support for Pierce. They even traveled to Concord to encourage him to actively campaign for the nomination.

Pierce told them he would accept the nomination only if the convention became deadlocked among the major contenders.

▶ Compromise of 1850

In May 1852, the editor of a Richmond, Virginia, newspaper sent all the presidential candidates a set of three questions. The questions were about the Compromise of 1850, which attempted to resolve the slavery issue and forestall the Civil War.

The three major provisions of the act were:

1. California would be admitted to the Union as a free (non-slavery) state.

2. The slave trade, but not slavery itself, in the District of Columbia was abolished.

3. The Fugitive Slave Law, which compelled the federal government to take an active part in returning escaped slaves to their masters, was strengthened.

◀ *Caleb Cushing.*

The strengthening of the Fugitive Slave Law was the most controversial part of the law. Suspected fugitive slaves were denied the right to a trial by jury. Because of that, it was possible for free blacks living in the North to be turned over to white Southerners who claimed they were runaway slaves.

In a carefully worded response, Pierce said that he supported the Compromise, but he was not expecting to be a candidate. He was in favor of the Compromise only as a measure to hold the Union together.

An Unlikely Candidate

The Democratic Convention was held in Baltimore on June 1, 1852. On the first ballot, Pierce was not even mentioned. Cass and Buchanan were the early leaders, but neither candidate could get the required two thirds of the delegate votes to win the nomination. On the thirtieth ballot, Douglas became the leading candidate. On the thirty-fifth, the lead shifted to Cass, and Pierce received his first votes. Finally, on the forty-ninth ballot, Pierce was chosen as a compromise candidate. Senator William Rufus King of Alabama was chosen as his running mate. The Democrats felt Pierce was a candidate that would carry on the legacy of former Democratic President Andrew Jackson. They even called Pierce "Young Hickory of the Granite Hills" in honor of Jackson, whose nickname had been Old Hickory.[2]

Millard Fillmore.

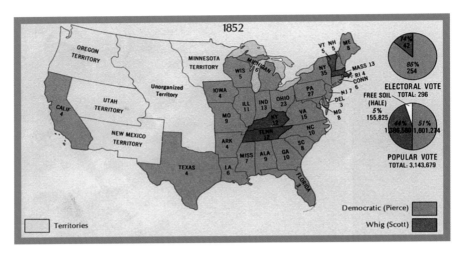

▲ This map shows the results of the presidential election of 1852.

The incumbent president, Millard Fillmore, was not renominated by the Whig Party. Instead the Whigs nominated General Winfield Scott, a commander of the United States forces in the Mexican War. Both candidates conducted a leisurely campaign. Scott made only one campaign trip through the western states. Pierce stayed in Concord greeting visitors and writing letters while Democratic Party leaders traveled and made speeches.

The Whigs played up General Scott's war record and accused Pierce of cowardice under fire during the Mexican War. The Democrats reminded voters that General Scott had once been court-martialed. Both parties accused the opposition's nominee of being a drunkard.

▶ A Puzzling Pierce

The most troublesome issue for Pierce was his position on the Fugitive Slave Law. It was reported that, in an 1851 speech, Pierce had characterized the law as inhumane and morally wrong. However, Pierce still maintained that the law should be enforced. That position puzzled and disturbed both Northerners and Southerners.

Pierce defended his position by claiming he had been misrepresented. He claimed that he had been "unwell" when he made the speech and that his rapid-fire, off-the-cuff delivery of the speech made it difficult for him to recall what he had said. Weak as it was, it was still better than no explanation.

When the votes were counted, Pierce won by an overwhelming vote in the electoral college. He carried twenty-seven of thirty-one states for an electoral victory of

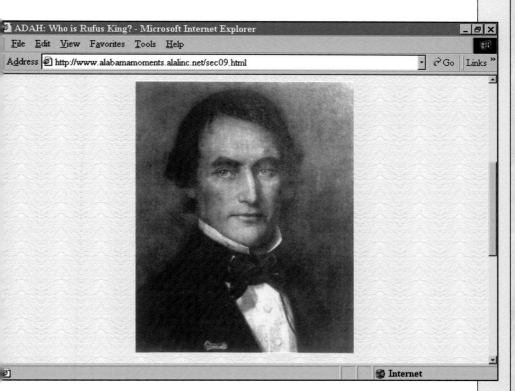

ADAH: Who is Rufus King? - Microsoft Internet Explorer

File   Edit   View   Favorites   Tools   Help

Address http://www.alabamamoments.alalinc.net/sec09.html   Go   Links »

Internet

▲ *William Rufus King is the only official to take the oath of office on foreign soil. By a special act of Congress, he was administered the oath of office in Cuba, while he was receiving treatment for tuberculosis. He died just a few months into the administration.*

254 to 42. Yet the popular vote was much closer. Out of over 3 million votes cast, Pierce had 1,601,474 votes to Scott's 1,386,578. The rest of the votes went to candidates of other parties such as the Free-Soil and Know-Nothing Parties. A slim majority of 51 percent of the voters cast their ballots for Pierce.

Midway between Election Day and Inauguration Day, a terrible tragedy would befall Franklin and Jane Pierce. It would cast a pall over them and put a terrible strain on their marriage.

Chapter 5

Presidency, 1853–1857

On the morning of January 6, 1853, Franklin, Jane, and their son, Benjamin, boarded a train in Boston bound for Concord, New Hampshire. The train had only traveled about one mile when it derailed and rolled down an embankment. Franklin and Jane were only slightly injured, but young Benjamin was killed.[1]

▶ A Tragic Loss

Eleven-year-old Benjamin had been their only surviving son. Their first child, Franklin, had died in infancy. A second son, Frank Robert, died when he was four. Franklin and Jane's hopes, dreams, and ambitions had been focused on their only surviving child.

Jane interpreted the tragic death as a sign from God that Pierce would have nothing to distract him from the presidency.[2] Pierce blamed himself for the tragedy. During most of her husband's presidency, Jane would seclude herself in her White House bedroom and write letters to her dear departed son. Pierce would have little, if any, strength and support from his wife while he was president.

▶ Building a "Compromise Cabinet"

After burying and grieving for his son, Pierce turned his attention to naming a Cabinet. Since he had been nominated as a compromise candidate, Pierce assembled what was called a compromise Cabinet. He tried to see that the North and South, and all factions of his party were represented.

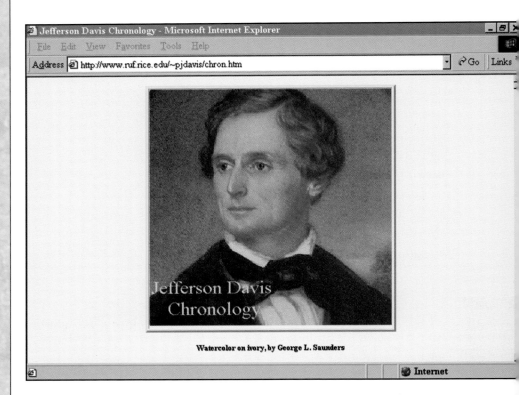

Jefferson Davis Chronology - Microsoft Internet Explorer

File   Edit   View   Favorites   Tools   Help

Address   http://www.ruf.rice.edu/~pjdavis/chron.htm   Go   Links

Jefferson Davis Chronology

Watercolor on ivory, by George L. Saunders

Internet

▲ *Senator Jefferson Davis served as Pierce's secretary of war in his compromise Cabinet.*

Mississippi Senator Jefferson Davis was chosen as secretary of war. The South was also represented by James Guthrie of Kentucky as secretary of the treasury, and James C. Dobbin of North Carolina as secretary of the Navy.

Northern Cabinet members included New Yorker William L. Marcy for secretary of state and Robert McClelland of Michigan for secretary of the interior. As a reward to the clique of Mexican War generals who had supported him, Pierce made General Caleb Cushing of Massachusetts his attorney general.

The End of Slavery?

On March 4, 1853, Franklin Pierce was inaugurated as the fourteenth president of the United States. He had memorized his inaugural address and delivered it without notes. President Pierce began his address by speaking in favor of trade expansion, economy in government, peace, and expanding the borders of the United States. Then, he spoke of slavery.

"I believe," Pierce said, "that involuntary servitude as it exists in different states of this Confederacy, is recognized by the Constitution. I believe that it stands like any other admitted right, and that the states where it exists are entitled

This picture depicts Pierce's inaugural parade on March 4, 1853.

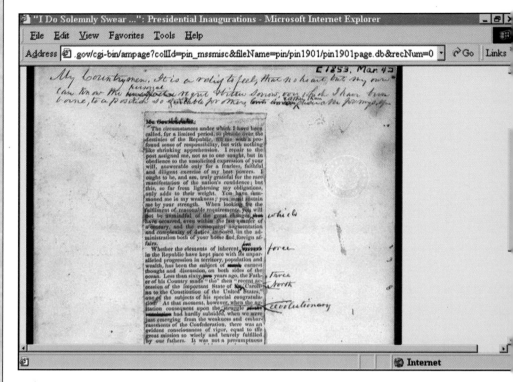

This document is a portion of Pierce's inaugural address, which he delivered on March 4, 1853.

to efficient remedies . . . I fervently hope that the question is at rest. . . ."[3]

If the new president truly believed that slavery would no longer be an issue, he was only fooling himself.

▶ The Gadsden Purchase

An early triumph for the Pierce administration was the Gadsden Purchase in 1853. Under this agreement, negotiated by U.S. Minister to Mexico James Gadsden, the United States purchased a 45,535-square-mile strip of land from Mexico.

The land was located in what is now southern Arizona and New Mexico. The purchase price was $10 million and it helped the Pierce administration achieve its goal of expanding the borders of the United States.

Opening of Japan

One of the most significant events of the Pierce administration was the opening of trade between the United States and Japan. Pierce's predecessor, President Millard Fillmore, had twice sent letters to the Japanese emperor, urging trade between the two nations. Acting as an emissary for ex-President Fillmore, Commodore Matthew Perry made two visits to Japan. During his second visit in March 1854, Perry induced Japan to sign the Treaty of Kanagawa. The treaty opened the ports of Shimoda and Hakodate for trade with United States ships. In 1856, the American flag was flown in Japan for the first time.

The Ostend Manifesto

Another attempt at expanding United States land holdings was an unfortunate embarrassment for President Pierce. He had hoped to expand the southern boundary of the United States by acquiring the island of Cuba from Spain. He authorized Secretary of State Marcy to negotiate the transaction. Marcy then told U.S. Minister to Spain Pierre Soulé that if Spain refused to sell, other means of acquisition were justifiable.

Soulé later met with U.S. Minister to France John Y. Mason and U.S. Minister to Great Britain James Buchanan. After meeting, the three drew up a document that came to be known as the Ostend Manifesto. The document asserted that the United States would be justified in going to war with Spain to acquire Cuba.

The document became public knowledge after it was leaked to, and published in, the *New York Herald*. Administration opponents criticized Pierce for even considering going to war to seize Cuba. He was further criticized by political opponents who saw it as a scheme to expand slavery. President Pierce and Secretary of State Marcy were finally compelled to repudiate the Ostend Manifesto.

However, the problems brought on by the Ostend Manifesto were insignificant compared to the perpetual controversy over slavery. Pierce's inability to resolve the issue doomed his administration.

▶ The Kansas-Nebraska Act

The Kansas-Nebraska Act has been called the great tragedy of the Pierce administration. The act was drafted by a Senate committee that was chaired by Stephen Douglas. The act provided that the residents of the Kansas and Nebraska territories would vote to decide if they would enter the Union as a free state or as a slave state. This idea was known as popular sovereignty. Because of the 1820 Missouri Compromise, the two territories had previously been closed to slavery.

President Pierce supported the act because he thought it was a fair and acceptable compromise between the North and South. He believed it was a pact that both Northerners and Southerners could live with.

Slavery was never really an issue in the Nebraska Territory. The residents there were overwhelmingly anti-slavery. Kansas was a different matter. Northerners settled there in hopes that the territory would be admitted as a free state. Pro-slavery "border ruffians" from Missouri also migrated to Kansas seeking to make it a slave state. The battle between the two factions would be prolonged, violent, and bloody.

"Bleeding Kansas"

The most infamous incident was on May 24, 1856, at Pottawatomie Creek. An abolitionist named John Brown led a raid in which five pro-slavery settlers were killed. There were other random acts of violence by both factions. The Kansas Territory came to be known as Bleeding Kansas. It is estimated that two hundred people were killed in the struggle between the antislavery and pro-slavery forces.

The violence in the Kansas Territory reached its peak in the spring of 1856. On May 21, the town of Lawrence was sacked by pro-slavery forces. Many homes were pillaged and the Free State Hotel was burned down. The offices and presses of two newspapers—*The Herald of Freedom* and *The Kansas Free State*—were destroyed. Although there

▲ *In the spring of 1856, an abolitionist named John Brown led a raid in which five pro-slavery settlers were killed. As a result, the Kansas Territory became known as Bleeding Kansas. This painting by John Steuart Curry is in the Kansas State Capital Building.*

was only one death, exaggerated accounts of the violence in Lawrence inflamed the sentiments of Northern anti-slavery activists.

In retaliation, on May 24–25, an antislavery fanatic named John Brown and six of his companions carried out the Pottawatomie Massacre. Five pro-slavery settlers were executed by Brown and his followers. The Kansas Territory was in a virtual state of civil war. Sporadic violence in Kansas continued throughout the Pierce administration. Kansas finally entered the Union as a free state in 1861.

The Know-Nothing Party

President Pierce's support of the Kansas-Nebraska Act cost him control of his party. In the 1854 midterm elections, the Democrats lost control of the House of Representatives to the new, antislavery Republican Party. Pierce also lost the support of Southern Democrats who were impatient and unhappy with his inability to pass other pro-South legislation after the Kansas-Nebraska Act. The rapid ascendancy of an anti-Catholic third party called the Know-Nothing Party further eroded President Pierce's political base.

A Blemished Reputation

Yet another blemish on the Pierce administration was his decision to recognize a pro-slavery rebel government in the Central American nation of Nicaragua. In 1855, a pro-slavery soldier of fortune named William Walker set up a rebel government in the civil-war-torn country. At first, Pierce refused to receive an emissary dispatched by Walker, but he later relented. Walker's regime ended in 1857, after Pierce had left office.

In June 1856, the Democrats held their national convention in Cincinnati. On the first ballot, President

Tools   Search   Notes   Discuss   Go!

Pierce narrowly trailed James Buchanan, 135 to 122. Pierce's support gradually eroded and drifted to Stephen Douglas. After sixteen ballots, Douglas withdrew and Buchanan became the Democratic Party's nominee for president. As a result, Pierce became the only elected president to seek his party's nomination and not receive it.[4]

After returning to Washington, President Pierce announced that he fully supported Buchanan's nomination. In November, Buchanan was elected to succeed Pierce as president. After watching Buchanan's inauguration on March 4, 1857, Franklin and Jane Pierce prepared to return to New Hampshire.

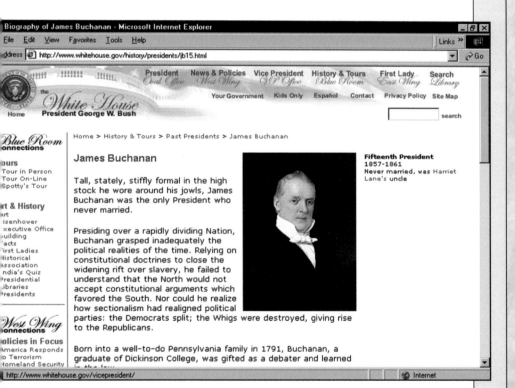

James Buchanan received the Democratic Party's nomination for president in the election of 1856.

Chapter 6

After the Presidency, 1857–1869

After James Buchanan was inaugurated, the Pierces stayed in Washington for a few more weeks. The weather in New Hampshire was too cold and harsh for Jane's delicate health. Franklin and Jane Pierce stayed at the home of former Secretary of State William Marcy.

The ex-president would enjoy a retirement free of financial worries. When they were in the White House, the Pierces had lived frugally. Pierce was able to save and invest half of his presidential salary. He had around $78,000 in savings and investments when he left office. This was a very large amount of money at that time.

▶ Years Abroad

For the past four years, Jane had suffered silently. She detested Washington, and she remained grief stricken over Bennie's tragic death. Now Pierce could give her his undivided attention. He hoped that a long European vacation would lift her spirits.

In the fall of 1857, the Pierces embarked on a lengthy vacation. They spent the winter on the Portuguese island of Madeira. Then they visited Portugal, Spain, France, Switzerland, Italy, Austria, Germany, Belgium, and England. While in Rome, Pierce enjoyed a joyous reunion with his old friend Nathaniel Hawthorne. Hawthorne noticed how the burden of the presidency had aged his dear friend. Pierce's face was deeply wrinkled and his hair was turning white.

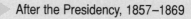

Tools   Search   Notes   Discuss   Go!

Pierce maintained his avid interest in American politics. He eagerly read newspapers and periodicals. He also corresponded with some of his former Cabinet members such as Jefferson Davis and Caleb Cushing. Pierce took some quiet satisfaction in learning that Buchanan was plagued by the same problems he had. The rift between the North and the South continued to grow and a war between the two regions seemed unavoidable.

In the summer of 1859, the Pierces returned to America. All of the traveling and sight-seeing had not banished Jane's mournful moods. She still obsessed over

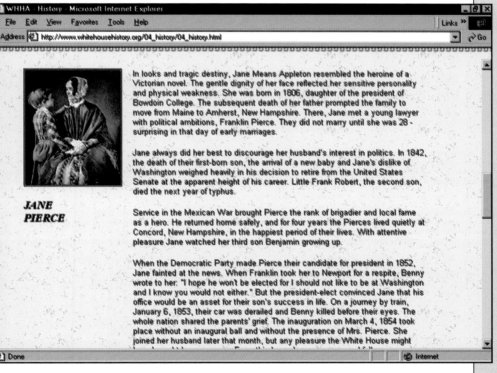

WHHA - History - Microsoft Internet Explorer

File   Edit   View   Favorites   Tools   Help   Links »

Address http://www.whitehousehistory.org/04_history/04_history.html   Go

JANE PIERCE

In looks and tragic destiny, Jane Means Appleton resembled the heroine of a Victorian novel. The gentle dignity of her face reflected her sensitive personality and physical weakness. She was born in 1806, daughter of the president of Bowdoin College. The subsequent death of her father prompted the family to move from Maine to Amherst, New Hampshire. There, Jane met a young lawyer with political ambitions, Franklin Pierce. They did not marry until she was 28 - surprising in that day of early marriages.

Jane always did her best to discourage her husband's interest in politics. In 1842, the death of their first-born son, the arrival of a new baby and Jane's dislike of Washington weighed heavily in his decision to retire from the United States Senate at the apparent height of his career. Little Frank Robert, the second son, died the next year of typhus.

Service in the Mexican War brought Pierce the rank of brigadier and local fame as a hero. He returned home safely, and for four years the Pierces lived quietly at Concord, New Hampshire, in the happiest period of their lives. With attentive pleasure Jane watched her third son Benjamin growing up.

When the Democratic Party made Pierce their candidate for president in 1852, Jane fainted at the news. When Franklin took her to Newport for a respite, Benny wrote to her: "I hope he won't be elected for I should not like to be at Washington and I know you would not either." But the president-elect convinced Jane that his office would be an asset for their son's success in life. On a journey by train, January 6, 1853, their car was derailed and Benny killed before their eyes. The whole nation shared the parents' grief. The inauguration on March 4, 1854 took place without an inaugural ball and without the presence of Mrs. Pierce. She joined her husband later that month, but any pleasure the White House might

Done   Internet

▲ *Jane Pierce is pictured with their son Bennie, who died in a train accident shortly before Pierce's inauguration. He was their third and only surviving child. The grieving parents blamed themselves for the tragedy and his death.*

the deaths of her three sons and the more recent deaths of her mother and sister.

Election of 1860

With the 1860 presidential election approaching, the Democrats looked for a compromise candidate that could unite the country. Cushing and some other politicians approached Pierce as a possible candidate. Pierce emphatically declined the offer. He was through with politics. Because of Jane's fragile state, a return to Washington was unthinkable.

While the Pierces vacationed in the tropical West Indies, the Republicans and Democrats held their national conventions. The Democrats broke off into two factions with two candidates. The moderate Democrats nominated Illinois Senator Stephen A. Douglas. The Southern Democrats chose Buchanan's vice president, John C. Breckenridge, as their nominee.

The Republicans nominated former Illinois Congressman Abraham Lincoln as their presidential candidate.

A Split in the Union

The party split allowed Lincoln to win a narrow victory. Before Lincoln was inaugurated, the Southern states seceded from the Union and formed the Confederate States of America (CSA). Their Congress chose Jefferson Davis as president.

Pierce's friends urged him to use his prestige as an ex-president to persuade the Southern states to stay in the Union. Pierce did write some letters asking his Southern friends to stay in the Union, but they had no effect. Pierce underestimated how strongly the South felt about protecting what they felt was part of the Southern way of life.

When war did break out, Pierce wrote ex-President Martin Van Buren and suggested that all the surviving ex-presidents (Van Buren, John Tyler, Millard Fillmore, Pierce, and Buchanan) meet in Philadelphia and make a plea for peace and national unity. Van Buren declined to convene the meeting, but he wrote Pierce and suggested that he do it. Nothing was done.

Pierce opposed the Southern states' right to secede from the Union, but he still felt slavery was legal. Apparently, he never thought it was wrong for one human being to own another. When President Lincoln issued the Emancipation Proclamation, Pierce criticized the act and declared that the Constitution had been overthrown.

On July 4, 1863, Pierce gave a speech at Concord, New Hampshire, denouncing President Lincoln and the Civil War. Pierce called the conflict a "fearful, fruitless, fatal civil war."[1] The speech alienated many of Pierce's friends and destroyed the prestige he had held as an ex-president.

▶ Quiet Last Days

Jane Pierce died on December 2, 1863. The following spring, Pierce's longtime friend Nathaniel Hawthorne died. Pierce attended the funeral and was snubbed by the other mourners. He was not asked to be a pallbearer at his friend's funeral.

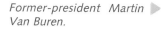
Former-president Martin ▶
Van Buren.

Franklin Pierce spent his last years quietly brooding. Most of the time he was alone. His few remaining friends did not visit. He died at his home in Concord on October 8, 1869.

Pierce is regarded as a weak president who was overwhelmed by events. During his administration, the slavery issue went from being a persistent problem to becoming a catalyst to war. However, even Pierce's detractors and opponents would concede that he was sincere and patriotic.

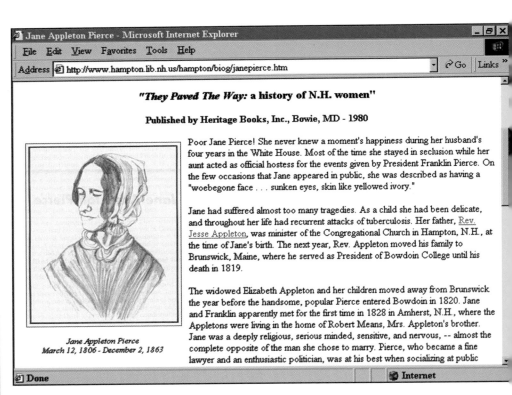

Jane Appleton Pierce - Microsoft Internet Explorer

File   Edit   View   Favorites   Tools   Help

Address http://www.hampton.lib.nh.us/hampton/biog/janepierce.htm   Go   Links

"*They Paved The Way:* a history of N.H. women"

Published by Heritage Books, Inc., Bowie, MD - 1980

Poor Jane Pierce! She never knew a moment's happiness during her husband's four years in the White House. Most of the time she stayed in seclusion while her aunt acted as official hostess for the events given by President Franklin Pierce. On the few occasions that Jane appeared in public, she was described as having a "woebegone face . . . sunken eyes, skin like yellowed ivory."

Jane had suffered almost too many tragedies. As a child she had been delicate, and throughout her life had recurrent attacks of tuberculosis. Her father, Rev. Jesse Appleton, was minister of the Congregational Church in Hampton, N.H., at the time of Jane's birth. The next year, Rev. Appleton moved his family to Brunswick, Maine, where he served as President of Bowdoin College until his death in 1819.

The widowed Elizabeth Appleton and her children moved away from Brunswick the year before the handsome, popular Pierce entered Bowdoin in 1820. Jane and Franklin apparently met for the first time in 1828 in Amherst, N.H., where the Appletons were living in the home of Robert Means, Mrs. Appleton's brother. Jane was a deeply religious, serious minded, sensitive, and nervous, -- almost the complete opposite of the man she chose to marry. Pierce, who became a fine lawyer and an enthusiastic politician, was at his best when socializing at public

Jane Appleton Pierce
March 12, 1806 - December 2, 1863

Done   Internet

▲ Jane Appleton Pierce was a frail and delicate woman as a result of chronic tuberculosis. She suffered many tragedies throughout her life, including the deaths of her three children. Her stay at the White House was a miserable one, as she disapproved of her husband's political activities and remained in seclusion.

Franklin Pierce's belief that slavery was tolerable, Constitutional, and not morally wrong tarnished his reputation. For years, the state of New Hampshire refused to honor his memory. Finally in 1895, a project to honor him was organized. Still, it was not until 1914 that a statue of Pierce was erected in Concord.

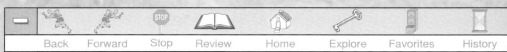
Chapter 1. Where is the Flag?, 1865

1. Roy Franklin Nichols, *Franklin Pierce: Young Hickory of the Granite Hills* (Philadelphia: University of Pennsylvania Press, 1958), p. 526.

2. Ibid.

3. Ibid.

Chapter 3. Politician & Attorney, 1828–1851

1. Paul F. Boller, Jr., *Presidential Anecdotes* (New York: Oxford University Press, 1981), p. 115.

2. Roy Franklin Nichols, *Franklin Pierce: Young Hickory of the Granite Hills* (Philadelphia: University of Pennsylvania Press, 1958), p. 172.

Chapter 4. Dark Horse Candidate, 1852

1. Roy Franklin Nichols, *Franklin Pierce: Young Hickory of the Granite Hills* (Philadelphia: University of Pennsylvania Press, 1958), p. 198.

2. Paul F. Boller, Jr., *Presidential Anecdotes* (New York: Oxford University Press, 1981), p. 114.

Chapter 5. Presidency, 1853–1857

1. Paul F. Boller, Jr., *Presidential Anecdotes* (New York: Oxford University Press, 1981), p. 115.

2. Ibid.

3. Roy Franklin Nichols, *Franklin Pierce: Young Hickory of the Granite Hills* (Philadelphia: University of Pennsylvania Press, 1958), pp. 235–236.

4. Joseph Nathan Kane, *Facts About the Presidents: From George Washington to Bill Clinton,* 6th ed. (New York: The H. W. Wilson Company, 1993), p. 85.

Chapter 6. After the Presidency, 1857–1869

1. Roy Franklin Nichols, *Franklin Pierce: Young Hickory of the Granite Hills* (Philadelphia: University of Pennsylvania Press, 1958), p. 522.

Further Reading

Brown, Fern G., and Richard G. Young, ed. *Franklin Pierce: Fourteenth President of the United States.* Ada, Okla.: Garrett Educational Corporation, 1989.

DeGregorio, William A. *The Complete Book of U.S. Presidents: From George Washington to Bill Clinton.* New York: Wings Books, 1997.

Gara, Larry. *The Presidency of Franklin Pierce.* Lawrence: University Press of Kansas, 1991.

Gould, Lewis L., ed. *American First Ladies: Their Lives and Legacy.* New York: Routledge, 2001.

Hawthorne, Nathaniel. *The Life of Franklin Pierce.* Portsmouth, N.H.: Peter E. Randall Publisher, 1992.

Jacobs, William J. *War with Mexico.* Brookfield, Conn.: Millbrook Press, Incorporated, 1993.

Lawson, Don. *The United States in the Mexican War.* New York: HarperCollins Children's Book Group, 1998.

Nardo, Don. *The Mexican-American War.* San Diego, Calif.: Lucent Books, 1999.

Nichols, Roy F., and Katherine E. Speirs, ed. *Franklin Pierce: Young Hickory of the Granite Hills.* Newtown, Conn.: American Political Biography, 1993.

Steins, Richard. *Taylor, Fillmore, Pierce, & Buchanan.* Vero Beach, Fla.: Rourke Corporation, 1996.

Welsbacher, Anne. *Franklin Pierce.* Minneapolis, Minn.: ABDO Publishing Company, 2001.

Young, Jeff C. *The Fathers of American Presidents.* Jefferson, N.C.: McFarland, 1997.

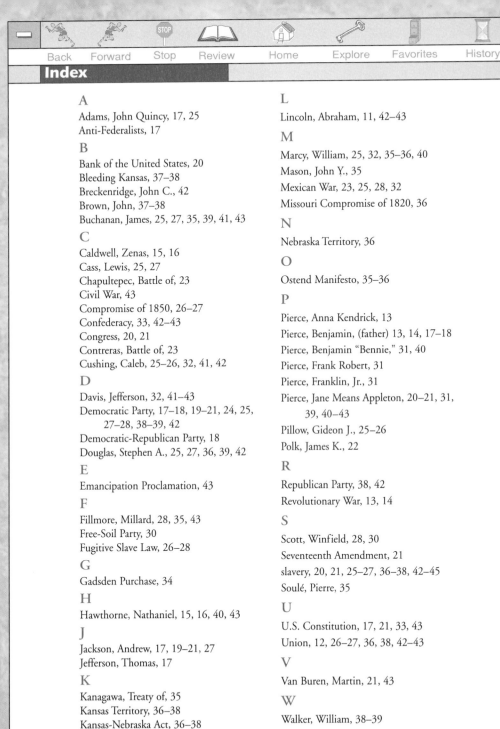

FOLGER McKINSEY ELEMENTARY SCHOOL